This book belongs to:

..................................................

Name

My First Eucharist:

..................................................

Date

..................................................

Parish

Jesus said to them, "I am the bread of life,
whoever comes to me will never hunger,
and whoever believes in me will never thirst....
I am the living bread that came down from heaven,
whoever eats this bread will live forever,
and the bread that I will give is my flesh
for the life of the world."

JOHN 6:35, 51

*Imprimi Potest:* Stephen T. Rehrauer, CSsR, Provincial,
Denver Province, the Redemptorists

*Imprimatur:* "In accordance with CIC 827, permission to publish has been granted on August 12, 2019, by the Most Reverend Mark S. Rivituso, Auxiliary Bishop, Archdiocese of St. Louis. Permission to publish is an indication that nothing contrary to Church teaching is contained in this work. It does not imply any endorsement of the opinions expressed in the publication; nor is any liability assumed by this permission."

Published by Liguori Publications, Liguori, Missouri 63057.
To order, call 800-325-9521, or visit Liguori.org.



ISBN: 978-0-7648-2824-9



Liguori Publications, a nonprofit corporation, is an apostolate of the Redemptorists (Redemptorists.com).

Design: Wendy Barnes
Illustrations: Jeff Albrecht

Printed in the United States of America • First Edition
20 21 22 23 24 / 5 4 3 2 1

**Dedication**

*Meet the Gentle Jesus* is dedicated to its editor, the gifted and inspiring Mary Wuertz von Holt, who blessed me with the original concept, encouraged me through the highs and lows of bringing it to fruition, and then lifted the content even higher with a keen eye for detail and a disciple's heart for meaning. Mary, your generosity knows no bounds, and I will never forget the joy of our collaboration!

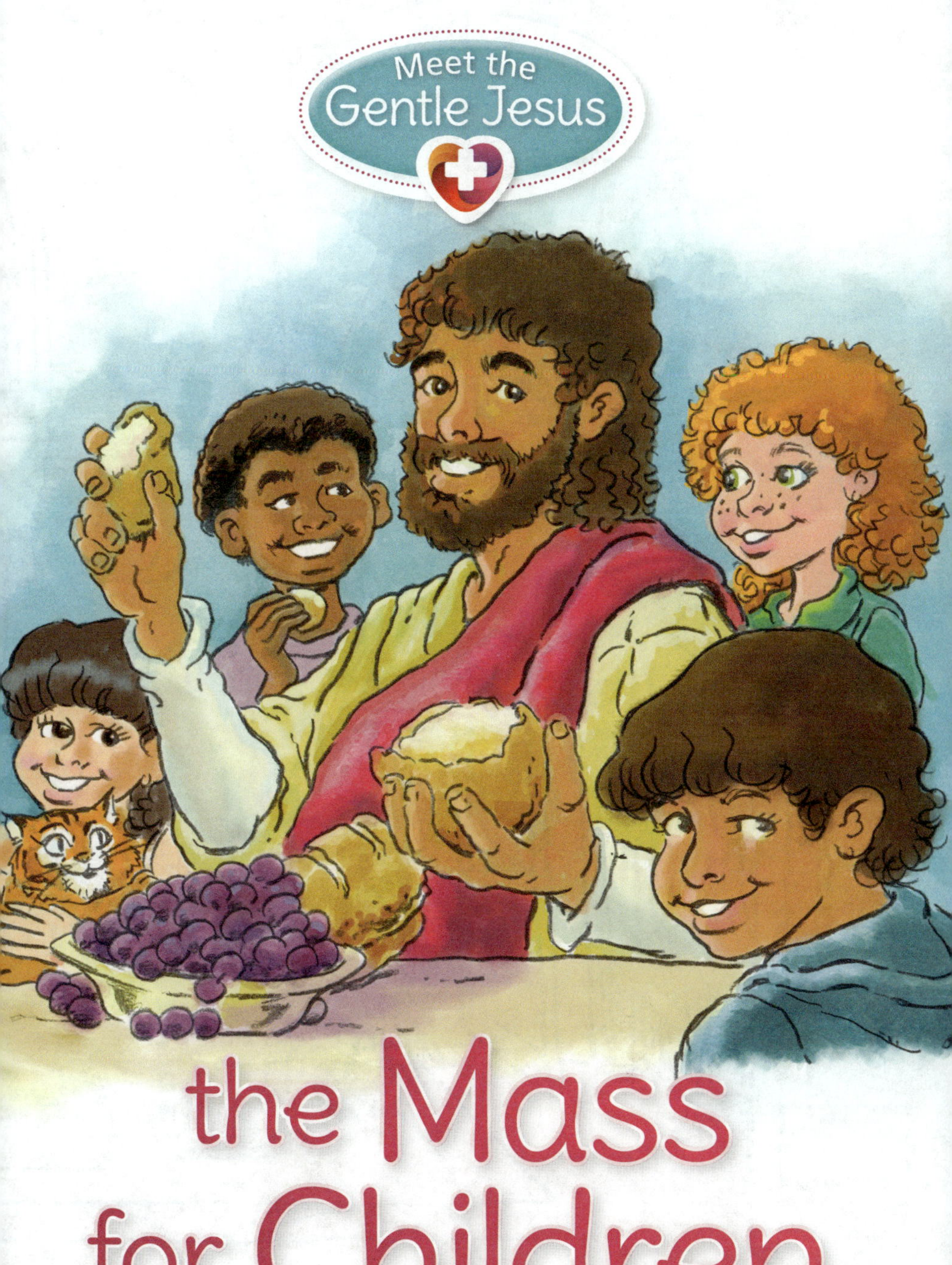


# the Mass for Children

Barbara Yoffie ⋆ Illustrated by Jeff Albrecht

1) Fourteenth Station of the Cross 2) Doors to Sacristy
3) Easter Candle 4) Ambo 5) Processional Cross

6) Crucifix 7) Tabernacle 8) Altar 9) Sanctuary Lamp
10) Lectern 11) Sanctuary 12) First Station of the Cross

## Before Mass

We gather to celebrate Mass because we belong to God's family. Here we meet the gentle Jesus who waits for us with open arms. We praise him and thank him.

### You Time

Look around the church. Do you see your friends and other people you know? You can smile and welcome them to Mass.

# Introductory Rites

## Entrance **Stand**

Mass begins with a song and a procession. The people in the procession have special parts in the Mass. We have a special part, too! We show our love for God by our prayers, our singing, and our actions.

**You Time**

Do you know the entrance songs at the Masses you go to? Use the songbook to help you sing along. Look at the people in the entrance procession. Watch the priest. He may kiss the altar before walking to his chair.

## Greeting

Make the sign of the cross with the priest when the entrance song ends. The sign of the cross reminds us of our baptism and that God is always with us. The priest greets us and makes us feel welcome. The priest chooses one of three greetings.

Priest: In the name of the Father, and of the Son, and of the Holy Spirit.

**All: Amen.**

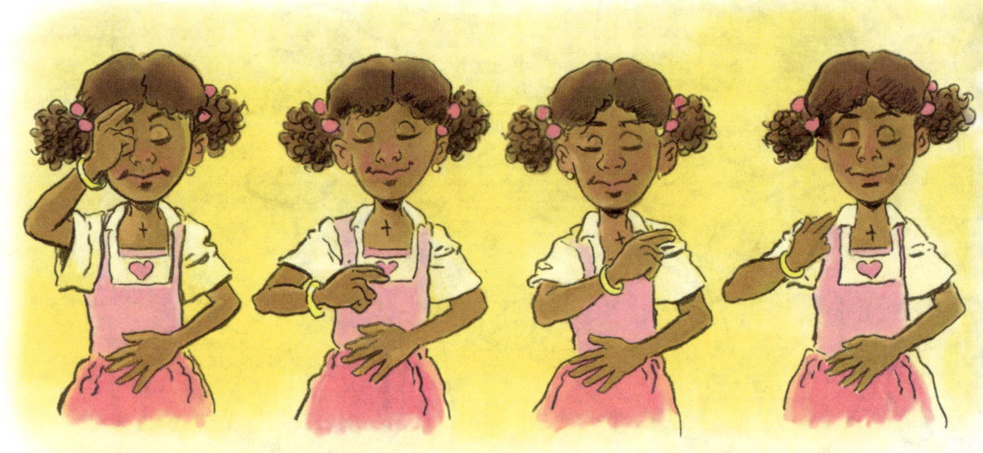

Priest: The grace of our Lord Jesus Christ, and the love of God, and the communion of the Holy Spirit be with you all.

OR

Priest: Grace to you and peace from God our Father and the Lord Jesus Christ.

OR

Priest: The Lord be with you.

**All: And with your spirit.**

## You Time

Practice making the sign of the cross with your right hand as you think about the Holy Trinity. Slowly touch your forehead (the Father), chest (the Son), left shoulder and right shoulder (and the Holy Spirit). Remember how much God loves you!

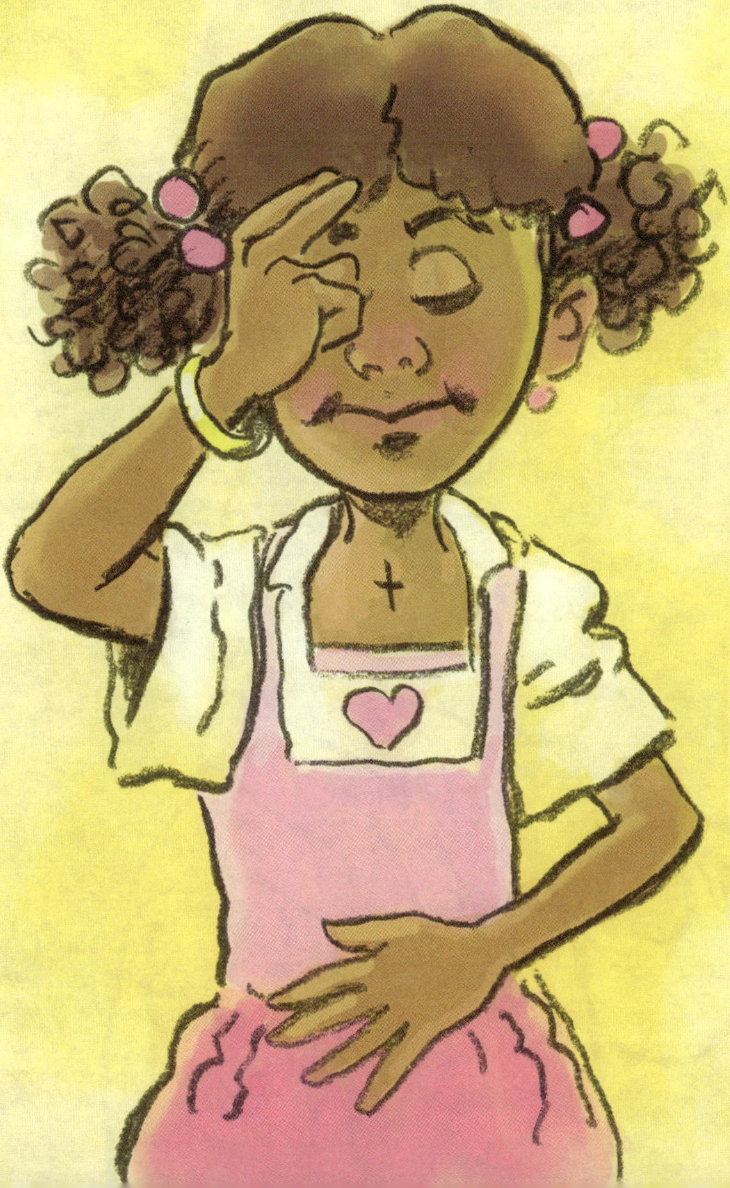

## Penitential Act

During the Penitential Act, we think of times when we have not loved God and others like we should. We ask God to forgive us and have mercy on us. We ask everyone in church to pray for us. God loves us and will forgive us. The priest chooses one of three prayers. These are the two most common prayers. And sometimes we are blessed with holy water to remind us of our baptism.

Do you remember a time when you hurt someone's feelings? Or a time when you did not tell the truth? How did you feel? What is the right thing to do? You should say you are sorry and ask for forgiveness. Be ready to forgive, like Jesus did, those who hurt you.

Priest: Brothers and sisters, let us acknowledge our sins, and so prepare ourselves to celebrate the sacred mysteries.

**All: I confess to almighty God**
**and to you, my brothers and sisters,**
**that I have greatly sinned,**
**in my thoughts and in my words,**
**in what I have done and in what I have failed to do,**
*(touch your heart with your right fist as you say...)*
**through my fault,**
**through my fault,**
**through my most grievous fault;**
**therefore I ask blessed Mary ever-Virgin,**
**all the Angels and Saints,**
**and you, my brothers and sisters,**
**to pray for me to the Lord our God.**

Priest: May almighty God have mercy on us,
forgive us our sins,
and bring us to everlasting life.

**All: Amen.**

OR

Priest or Deacon: You were sent to heal the contrite of heart: Lord, have mercy.

**All: Lord, have mercy.**

Priest or Deacon: You came to call sinners: Christ, have mercy.

**All: Christ, have mercy.**

Priest or Deacon: You are seated at the right hand of the Father to intercede for us: Lord, have mercy.

**All: Lord, have mercy.**

Priest: May almighty God have mercy on us,
forgive us our sins,
and bring us to everlasting life.

**All: Amen.**

## The Kyrie Eleison

*Kyrie Eleison* are Greek words that mean "Lord, have mercy."

Priest: Lord, have mercy. **All: Lord, have mercy.**
Or: Kyrie, eleison. **Or: Kyrie, eleison.**

Priest: Christ, have mercy. **All: Christ, have mercy.**
Or: Christe, eleison. **Or: Christe, eleison.**

Priest: Lord, have mercy. **All: Lord, have mercy.**
Or: Kyrie, eleison. **Or: Kyrie, eleison.**

## The Gloria: Glory to God

The Gloria is a special prayer of praise! God is so good to us! We want to praise him and thank him. We pray or sing the Gloria at Sunday Mass and on special occasions. (During Advent and Lent, we do not pray or sing the Gloria at most Sunday or weekday Masses.)

"Glory to God in the highest, and on earth peace to people of good will." This is the song the angels sang when Jesus was born. Is your heart full of love for God? Pray or sing the Gloria with joy and enthusiasm. Think of ways you can give praise or thanks to God when you are not at Mass. Say this simple prayer, "Gentle Jesus, I praise your holy name."

**All:** Glory to God in the highest,
and on earth peace to people of good will.
we praise you,
we bless you,
we adore you,
we glorify you,
we give you thanks for your great glory
Lord God, heavenly King,
O God, almighty Father.

Lord Jesus Christ, Only Begotten Son,
Lord God, Lamb of God, Son of the Father,
you take away the sins of the world,
have mercy on us;
you take away the sins of the world,
receive our prayer;
you are seated at the right hand of the Father,
have mercy on us.
For you alone are the Holy One,
you alone are the Lord,
you alone are the Most High,
Jesus Christ,
with the Holy Spirit,
in the glory of God the Father. Amen.

## Collect

The Collect is the opening prayer. The priest invites everyone to pray, and after a short silence, he offers a special prayer to God for us. See how he opens his arms just as Jesus does.

Priest: Let us pray.

The priest says a short prayer. Then we respond.

**All: Amen.**

**You Time**

**After the priest says, "Let us pray," think of someone or something special that you would like to pray for during Mass. Close your eyes and say a prayer to God. God hears all the prayers you hold in your heart.**

# The Liturgy of the Word

## Sit

The readings we hear at Mass are from the Bible. On Sundays and special days we have two readings, a psalm, and the Gospel. A psalm is a song of praise. At Mass during the week we listen to one reading, a psalm, and the Gospel.

Now we sit so we can listen to some special stories. We hear stories about God. We hear stories about Jesus. The stories tell us how he loves and cares for us. The stories help us grow in our faith so we can follow Jesus. What can you do today to follow Jesus?

## First Reading

At the end of the reading, the lector says:

The word of the Lord.

**All: Thanks be to God.**

## Responsorial Psalm

After each psalm verse, we sing or pray the refrain.

## Second Reading

At the end of the reading, the lector says:

The word of the Lord.

**All: Thanks be to God.**

## Gospel Acclamation

**Stand**

We stand and sing the Gospel Acclamation. We sing a joyful Alleluia, which means "Praise God!" (During Lent we use a different response.) The Gospel is an important part of the Mass. The Gospel is a story about Jesus, how he lived, and what he taught. It is from one of the four evangelists, Matthew, Mark, or Luke, and on special days, John.

**All: Alleluia.**

Before the Gospel is read, with the thumb of your right hand trace the sign of the cross on your forehead, your lips, and your heart. Pray, "Jesus, be on my mind, in my words, and always in my heart." The Gospel is the "Good News" of Jesus. Think about the "Good News" Jesus shared with you in today's Gospel.

## Gospel

Priest or Deacon: The Lord be with you.

**All: And with your spirit.**

Priest or Deacon: A reading from the holy Gospel according to …

+ Trace the sign of the cross on your forehead, your lips, and your heart while you say:

**All: Glory to you, O Lord.**

At the end of the Gospel the priest or deacon says:
The Gospel of the Lord.

**All: Praise to you, Lord Jesus Christ.**

## Homily

### Sit

Everyone sits and listens to the homily. The priest or deacon talks about the readings. He helps us to understand how God is always with us and how much God loves us. In the homily, God speaks to each one of us so we can grow in holiness and faith.

God has a special message for everyone. Listen closely to the homily and talk with your parents after Mass. Tell them what you heard and remember. Talk about ways your family can put the messages of the homily into action.

## Profession of Faith (The Nicene Creed)

### Stand

On Sundays and special days we stand for the Profession of Faith. Encouraged by the readings and the homily, we pray the Creed. Usually we pray the Nicene Creed, though sometimes we pray the shorter Apostles' Creed. With both creeds, we proudly tell everyone what we believe as Catholics.

Our Catholic faith is very important. We show people we believe in the Blessed Trinity—Father, Son, and Holy Spirit—by how we live. Share your faith with others this week through kind words or helpful actions. You can make a difference!

**All: I believe in one God,**
**the Father almighty,**
**maker of heaven and earth,**
**of all things visible and invisible.**

**I believe in one Lord Jesus Christ,**
**the Only Begotten Son of God,**
**born of the Father before all ages.**
**God from God, Light from Light,**
**true God from true God,**
**begotten, not made, consubstantial with the Father;**
**through him all things were made.**
**for us men and for our salvation**
**he came down from heaven,**

*(for the following, we bow)*
**and by the Holy Spirit was incarnate of the Virgin Mary,**
**and became man.** *(stand up straight)*

**For our sake he was crucified under Pontius Pilate,**
**he suffered death and was buried,**
**and rose again on the third day**
**in accordance with the Scriptures.**
**He ascended into heaven**
**and is seated at the right hand of the Father.**
**He will come again in glory**
**to judge the living and the dead**
**and his kingdom will have no end.**

I believe in the Holy Spirit, the Lord, the giver of life,
who proceeds from the Father and the Son,
who with the Father and the Son is adored and glorified,
who has spoken through the prophets.

I believe in one, holy, catholic and apostolic Church.
I confess one Baptism for the forgiveness of sins
and I look forward to the resurrection of the dead
and the life of the world to come. Amen.

## Universal Prayer

### (also called Prayer of the Faithful or Petitions)

We offer special prayers to God and ask for his help. We pray for the Church, leaders of the world, and the special needs of our parish and community. When we pray for others we show our care and concern.

At the end of each petition the deacon or reader says:

We pray to the Lord.

OR

Let us pray to the Lord.

**All: Lord, hear our prayer.**

After all the petitions are read, the priest says a closing prayer. Then we respond.

**All: Amen.**

Prayer brings us closer to God. We can pray for God's help anytime or anywhere. You can pray for other people, too! Listen to each petition and respond, "Lord, hear our prayer." Add your own silent petition for a special person or need.

# Liturgy of the Eucharist

**Sit**

## Presentation of the Gifts
(or Preparation of the Altar)

It is time to prepare the altar. Sometimes we sing a song. The ushers collect money envelopes. People carry gifts of bread and wine to the priest or deacon; they carry the gifts to the altar. We offer all these things to God. We offer ourselves and our lives to God because we love him.

What will you offer to God? Remember, you can offer him anything: your joys and sorrows, a prayer or kind act. Listen to the priest as he asks God to accept our gifts. Be ready to answer him in prayer.

1) The Roman Missal
2) Cruets of Water and Wine
3) Finger Towel
4) Communion Host 5) Paten
6) Purificator 7) Chalice 8) Corporal

## Prayer Over the Offerings

The priest offers prayers of thanksgiving to God for the bread and wine. He may say them silently or, when there is no music, he may say them aloud.

**All: Blessed be God for ever.**

After the priest washes his hands, he prays:

Priest: Pray, brothers and sisters, that my sacrifice and yours may be acceptable to God, the almighty Father.

**Stand**

**All: May the Lord accept the sacrifice at your hands**
**for the praise and glory of his name,**
**for our good and the good of all his holy Church.**

The priest says a short prayer asking God to accept our offerings. Then we respond.

**All: Amen.**

## Eucharistic Prayer

### Stand

Eucharist is a word that means "Thanksgiving." The Eucharistic Prayer gives thanks and praise to God. We ask God to bless us, too. We honor God by saying or singing the "Holy, Holy, Holy."

Priest: The Lord be with you.

**All: And with your spirit.**

Priest: Lift up your hearts.

**All: We lift them up to the Lord.**

Priest: Let us give thanks to the Lord our God.

**All: It is right and just.**

The priest says a short prayer.

The Eucharistic Prayer is a long prayer, but a very important one. We thank God! We praise God! Say or sing the "Holy, Holy, Holy," with everyone in church and the angels and saints in heaven.

## The Sanctus (or the Holy, Holy, Holy)

**All: Holy, Holy, Holy Lord God of hosts.**
**Heaven and earth are full of your glory.**
**Hosanna in the highest.**
**Blessed is he who comes in the name of the Lord.**
**Hosanna in the highest.**

## Consecration

**Kneel**

We kneel to show respect. The priest asks God to send the Holy Spirit. Through the Holy Spirit the gifts of bread and wine are changed. They become the Body and Blood of Jesus Christ. We believe he is really present and with us. Together we proclaim what we believe.

**This is the most holy part of the Mass and a great miracle! The priest acts and speaks like Jesus at the Last Supper. Pretend that you are there with Jesus. The priest raises the host and then the chalice. Listen to his words.**

Priest: Take this all of you, and eat of it:
For this is my body
which will be given up for you.

Take this, all of you, and drink from it:
for this is the chalice of my blood,
the blood of the new and eternal covenant,
which will be poured out for you and for many
for the forgiveness of sins.

Do this in memory of me.

## The Mystery of Faith

Priest: The mystery of faith.

**All: We proclaim your Death, O Lord,**
**and profess your Resurrection**
**until you come again.**

OR

**All: When we eat this Bread and drink this Cup,**
**we proclaim your Death, O Lord,**
**until you come again.**

OR

**All: Save us, Savior of the world**
**For by your Cross and Resurrection**
**You have set us free.**

## Doxology and Great Amen

The Eucharistic Prayer continues. The priest reminds us of all the things Jesus did. He prays for the whole Church and other people. He also asks all the saints in heaven to pray with and for us. He raises the host and the chalice and speaks or sings of God's glory.

Priest: Through him, and with him, and in him,
O God, almighty Father,
in the unity of the Holy Spirit,
all glory and honor is yours,
for ever and ever.

**All: Amen.**

Sometimes you get so excited you want to shout or cheer. "Amen" means "so be it" or "it is true." Our prayer of praise deserves a great cheer! All our voices join together. We say or sing "Amen" with great joy in our hearts.

## The Communion Rite

### Stand

The priest opens his arms and invites all to pray the Lord's Prayer or Our Father together. We pray for our daily bread and we pray for forgiveness. We are getting ready to receive Jesus Christ in the Eucharist.

### You Time

Jesus taught the Our Father to his disciples. It is a prayer most of us know by heart. When we pray this prayer we think of ways we can follow Jesus. We think about other people and how we should treat them. Do you treat others with kindness like Jesus?

## The Lord's Prayer

**All: Our Father, who art in heaven,**
**hallowed be thy name;**
**thy kingdom come,**
**thy will be done on earth as it is in heaven.**
**Give us this day our daily bread;**
**and forgive us our trespasses**
**as we forgive those who trespass**
**against us;**
**and lead us not into temptation,**
**but deliver us from evil.**

Priest: Deliver us, Lord, we pray, from every evil,
graciously grant peace in our days,
that, by the help of your mercy,
we may be always free from sin
and safe from all distress,
as we await the blessed hope
and the coming of our Savior, Jesus Christ.

**All: For the kingdom,**
**the power and the glory are yours**
**now and forever. Amen.**

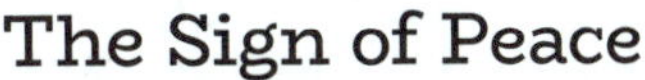

## The Sign of Peace

Jesus said, "Peace be with you." Jesus gives us his peace. He wants us to be friendly and kind, and to get along with people. We can share his peace with others.

Priest: The peace of the Lord be with you always.

**All: And with your spirit.**

Priest or Deacon: Let us offer each other the sign of peace.

Smile and shake hands with people near you. The peace of Jesus that is in your heart can be shared with everyone. How are you a peacemaker in your home, neighborhood, and school?

## Lamb of God

We say or sing the Lamb of God as the priest breaks the large host into small pieces. Jesus broke bread and gave it to his disciples at the Last Supper. The Lamb of God is Jesus Christ who gives himself to us in the Eucharist.

The priest raises the host and chalice, now the Body and Blood of Jesus Christ. Think about receiving Jesus into your heart. Pray, "Thank you, Jesus, for loving me so much. Help me to love you more each day."

**All:** **Lamb of God,**
**you take away the sins of the world,**
**have mercy on us.**

**Lamb of God,**
**you take away the sins of the world,**
**have mercy on us.**

**Lamb of God,**
**you take away the sins of the world,**
**grant us peace.**

## Kneel

Priest: Behold the Lamb of God,
behold him who takes away
the sins of the world,
Blessed are those called
to the supper of the Lamb.

**All:** **Lord, I am not worthy**
**that you should enter under my roof,**
**but only say the word**
**and my soul shall be healed.**

## Communion

### Kneel

The Communion song begins. We fold our hands and walk forward to receive the Body and Blood of Christ. We may receive Jesus Christ on our tongue or in our hands. If offered, we may drink the Precious Blood from the chalice. We feel very close to Jesus and to one another.

Priest, Deacon, or Extraordinary Minister:
The Body of Christ.

**All: Amen.**

Priest, Deacon, or Extraordinary Minister:
The Blood of Christ.

**All: Amen.**

To show your love for Jesus, bow your head before you receive the host (and drink from the chalice.) Jesus Christ gives you a great gift! He feeds you with his Body and Blood and fills your heart with love. Jesus wants you to share his love with others.

## Prayer after Communion

After everyone has received Communion, the priest or deacon and altar servers clear away everything used for our holy meal. Then the priest returns to his chair and we silently pray. Sometimes we sing a song. The priest prays that God will help us follow Jesus in our daily lives.

Priest: Let us pray.

**Stand**

The priest says a short prayer. Then we respond.

**All: Amen.**

Close your eyes and talk to Jesus in the silence of your heart. Be thankful. Ask Jesus to fill you with his gentleness and love.

# The Concluding Rites

### Stand

Sometimes the priest or deacon shares news about what is happening in the parish. The priest greets and then blesses the people. Sometimes we bow our heads for a special blessing. God's blessing helps us to grow in holiness.

God's blessing also strengthens us to do good things for others. During the week take time to think about the needs of other people. With God's help you can reach out and lend a helping hand!

## Greeting and Blessing

Priest: The Lord be with you.

**All: And with your spirit.**

Priest: May almighty God bless you,
the Father, and the Son,
and the Holy Spirit.

**All: Amen.**

## Dismissal

The word Mass means "sending." At the end of Mass, the priest or deacon sends all of us on a special mission. Go! Go out to do the good works of Jesus in the world!

We heard God's word. We were fed with the Body and Blood of Jesus Christ. We share God's love by our words and actions. How will you spread God's message? What will you do to help others like Jesus did?

Priest or Deacon: Go forth, the Mass is ended.

OR

Go and announce the Gospel of the Lord.

OR

Go in peace, glorifying the Lord by your life.

OR

Go in peace.

**All: Thanks be to God.**

It is time to leave our celebration. Sometimes we sing a joyful song. The priest and deacon kiss the altar and follow the servers in the procession.

They lead us into the world to be the heart and hands of the gentle Jesus.

# Glossary

**altar:** The central table on which the Communion bread and the cup of wine are offered as the eucharistic sacrifice. The altar "represents the two aspects of the same mystery: the altar of the sacrifice and the table of the Lord" (*CCC* 1383).

**ambo:** An elevated pulpit from which the Scriptures are proclaimed during Mass.

**baptismal font:** A large basin or small pool that contains the blessed water used for baptizing. Every parish church should have a baptismal font, which is usually set in a prominent and visible place in the church building.

**crucifix:** A cross with the image of Jesus as suffering Savior. Catholics find the blessed crucifix a revered object of private or public devotion as a reminder of the triumphant suffering of Christ.

**Easter candle:** A large candle symbolic of the risen Savior, the Light of the World. It is blessed on Holy Saturday and remains lit throughout the Easter season during liturgical services. It is also called the **paschal candle**.

**genuflect:** The action of briefly kneeling with one knee on the floor and blessing yourself with the Sign of the Cross while facing the tabernacle.

**holy water:** Water that is blessed by a priest for use by Catholics. It is used most often to make the Sign of the Cross while blessing oneself. Holy water is a reminder of baptism and symbolic of spiritual cleansing.

**lectern:** A wood or metal podium from which all nonscriptural readings and singing are led.

**pew:** The long bench you sit on during Mass. All pews in the church should face the altar.

**reconciliation room** or **confessional:** The place in a church set aside for celebration of the sacrament of penance. The penitent has the option of confessing to the priest face to face or anonymously behind a screen.

***Roman Missal, The*****:** Also called the ***Sacramentary***, this is a book of prayers and directives for the celebration of the Mass and other sacraments.

**sacristy:** A room near the sanctuary used to store sacred vessels and other materials used in the liturgy. This room is also used by the priest and other church ministers to prepare for Mass and other services.

**sanctuary:** The holy space around the altar, which may be a free-standing platform in the middle of the room, or it may be against the front wall. If it is in the front, normally it faces the east, in the direction of the rising sun/Son.

**sanctuary lamp:** A light or candle kept burning at all times whenever the Blessed Sacrament is present. This light can usually be found near the tabernacle.

**Stations of the Cross:** A series of pictures, carvings, or plaques found along the inside walls of the church representing events in the suffering and death of Jesus. These are used for prayer and meditation, especially during the season of Lent.

**tabernacle:** The tabernacle is the special place where the consecrated Eucharist is kept. It is located in a visible and prominent place in the church. You should genuflect before the tabernacle.

**vestments:** Symbolic garments worn by priests and deacons during liturgical celebrations.

A Picture to Color